PRO SPORTS
How Did They Begin?

Don L. Wulffson

illustrations by Alfred Giuliani

D1444950

For Gary Seidman, my sports buddy
from the time we were kids
—D. L. W.

For Mom, who I know is looking down from above
—A. D. G.

Photo Credits: © Bettmann/CORBIS: front cover (middle and lower right), p. 1 (left and center), p. 12, p. 20, p. 33, p. 35, p. 46, p. 50, p. 52, p. 54, p. 57; © Hulton-Deutsch Collection/CORBIS: front cover (lower left), p. 1 (right), p. 39, p. 44, back cover; © Schenectady Museum, Hall of Electrical History Foundation/CORBIS: front cover (top), p. 16; © TriaGiovan/CORBIS: p. 8; © CORBIS: p. 22; © Underwood & Underwood/CORBIS: p. 23, p. 42; © AP Photo: p. 37; © S. Carmona/CORBIS: p. 61

Text copyright © 2000 by Don L. Wulffson

For information contact:
MONDO Publishing
980 Avenue of the Americas
New York, New York 10018
Visit our website at http://www.mondopub.com

Printed in the United States of America
09 10   9 8 7 6 5 4

Cover design by NeuStudio
Interior design by Alfred Giuliani
Photo research by Sylvia P. Bloch

Library of Congress Cataloging-in-Publication Data

Wulffson, Don L.

    Pro sports : how did they begin? / Don L. Wulffson.
      p. cm.
    Summary: Presents historical facts and anecdotes about baseball, basketball, football, the three most popular professional sports in the U.S.

ISBN 1-57255-814-8

    1. Sports--United States--History--Juvenile literature. [1. Sports--History.] I. Title.
GV705.4.W84   2000
796.04'4'0973--dc21   00-021882

INTRODUCTION

The three most popular pro sports in the United States are football, basketball, and baseball. Some of the facts about what these sports were like in their early days sound impossible:

- Originally, there were no innings in baseball.

- The first basketball was a football.

- The first helmet worn by pro football players could be folded up and put in a back pocket.

The following pages explain how such things were possible. It is the story of what pro baseball, basketball, and football were like in the beginning, and how they slowly evolved into the games we know today.

PRO BASEBALL

Baseball is the oldest professional sport in the United States. And of any pro game, it has some of the wackiest and weirdest moments imaginable. For instance, there's the player who reached second, then decided to steal *first* base! Another genius is the batter who hit a homer, then ran the bases the wrong way! And not to be forgotten is Mike Grady who holds the distinction of being the only player to commit four errors on a single play!

Bonehead blunders and harebrained happenings—the annals of pro baseball are filled with them. They're great to read about. And so is the whole story of how the sport came to be.

A Kid's Game

Baseball was invented by boys and girls living in England in the early 1800s. "Rounders" is what they called the game. In rounders, a ball of solid rubber or tightly wound yarn was used, and the bat was a heavy stick. There was just one base—and it was a large wooden stake in the ground. The object of the game was to whack the ball as far as possible and then run around the stake and head for home. If a ball was caught on the fly, it was an out. It was also an out if the ball was caught *on one bounce*! Or, the runner could be "plugged." This meant that, incredibly, another way to make an out was to throw the ball and hit the runner!

You can probably figure out how rounders got its name changed to baseball. Kids pulled up the stake, tossed it, and used a base instead. More bases were added. By the year 1842, there were four bases, not three as there are today. Instead of running all the way back to home plate, the runner scored by reaching fourth base!

Here's what the field looked like:

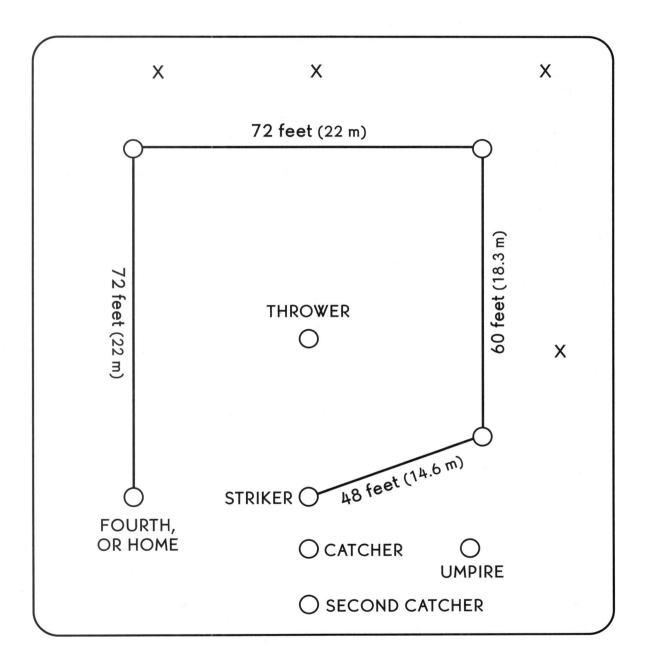

Grown-Ups Get Into the Game

By the late 1830s in the United States, adults had started playing baseball. At first, like the kids, they played just for fun. There were no uniforms; players wore whatever they wanted—usually long pants, long-sleeved shirts, ordinary street shoes, and straw hats. Runs were called aces. There were no innings; instead, the first team to score 21 aces was the winner. Players were known as "scouts," and there were 12 on each team—including four outfielders and *two catchers*, one behind the other. The reason for the second catcher was that there were no backstops in the early years of the game; not until 1879 did teams begin putting a screen behind home plate.

Another thing that was missing in the early 1800s was the stadium. Usually, there weren't even any stands; spectators just sat on the grass. The only person who had a place to sit was the umpire. And believe it or not, the custom was for him to sit in a rocking chair! Rocking away, he called it the way he saw it. "Strike four, yer outta there!" he'd yell. Or, "Ball nine, take yer base!" It sounds silly, but those were the rules in the early 1800s: It took four strikes, not three, to make an out. To get a "walk" to first base, it took nine off-target pitches.

Play-for-Pay Ball

July 20, 1858, was an important date for baseball. On that day, two New York teams played each other, and for the first time ever an admission fee was charged to watch the game. Fifty cents—that's all it cost. But it was the beginning of pro baseball.

In 1869, Harry Wright, a businessman and ballplayer, organized the first all-salaried pro team. Today, they're the Cincinnati Reds; in 1869, they were called the Cincinnati Red Stockings. The highest paid player on the team was none other than Harry Wright. He paid himself what was then a whopping good wage: $1,400 a season. Harry's brother, George Wright, had the second-highest salary: $1,200 a season.

Civil War Ball

The U.S. Civil War (1861–1865) could have killed pro baseball. And for the first couple of years of the war, interest in the game fizzled in the face of more important matters. But in the long run, the war did a great deal to change the game and increase Americans' interest in the sport.

It was in northern cities like New York, Boston, and Cincinnati that baseball was first played. Between battles, Union soldiers from these cities passed the time by playing ball. And they taught the game to Union soldiers from other states—Pennsylvania, Ohio, Indiana, Michigan, and Illinois.

Eventually, some of these soldiers were captured and put in Confederate prisoner-of-war camps in the South. There, the prisoners taught their southern guards the game. By war's end, baseball was being played all over America.

Baseball After the War

The Civil War led to many other changes, especially in what the players wore.

First, players tossed their straw hats. Instead, they began wearing the visored caps of Union soldiers. In time, these evolved into modern baseball caps.

During the Civil War, soldiers from the South wore gray uniforms and those from the North wore blue. This idea of distinctive, different-colored uniforms carried over from the battlefield to the baseball field. Before the war, some teams did not wear uniforms while others wore uniforms so similar in color and design that it was almost impossible to tell the two teams apart. After the war, it became a rule that each team had to have its own easily identifiable outfit.

Baseball uniform and equipment of the Civil War era

Did You Know?

In 1877, a rule was adopted by the National League that allowed club owners to deduct $30 from a player's annual salary toward the expense of his uniform.

The 1870s—Rules of Play

By the 1870s, baseball had evolved into a brand-new game. Still, it was different in many ways from the game played today. For example:

◆ The pitcher threw from just 45 feet (13.7 m) away from home base (instead of today's 60 feet, 6 inches [18.4 m]). He did not throw from a mound, but from a level, 6-foot (1.8 m)-square box. The batter stood with one foot on each side of a line drawn through home plate, and he had the right to call for a pitch above or below the waist! Imagine a modern-day pro player going up to bat and asking the pitcher to put the ball in his favorite place!

◆ The most important changes to the rules were those concerned with "balls" and "strikes." During the era of the 1870s, the number of strikes needed to get a batter out was lowered from four to three. Other rules of the time, however, made it extremely difficult for the pitcher to get strikes. Foul balls did not count as strikes. Stranger yet, the first good pitch a batter took was not called a strike, either! Rather, the umpire would warn the batter that he had to swing if the next pitch was in the strike zone.

◆ The pitchers received weird warnings from the umpire, as well. Incredibly, a pitch that was not called a strike was not automatically a ball; instead, the umpire would warn a pitcher several times that he had to throw "good, fair pitches" or he would begin calling balls. Once the umpire began calling balls and strikes, it took only three bad pitches—not four—for the batter to draw a walk.

◆ Foul rules! In the 1870s, a ball that touched fair territory and then spun foul was considered fair. So was a ball that was hit into the plate. Back in those days, home plate was actually a plate of iron. Hitters would try to bang a pitch straight down on the plate and send the ball ricocheting wildly off into foul territory. Such a hit was considered "fair," and the batter could run the

bases while the other team chased down the ball.

Pro Leagues

NAPBP. The first pro baseball league, formed in 1871, was the National Association of Professional Baseball Players. It was much like a workers' union. The players made the rules—and made most of the money. The team owners had almost no say in anything.

The National League. The National League, formed in 1876, was just the opposite. The owners took control of every aspect of the game. During the days of the NAPBP, players went around playing for any team they wanted—usually for whichever team would pay them the most. In a single season, a player would play for as many as ten different teams! The creation of the National League put a stop to this. In fact, it made it impossible for players to change teams. The contract guaranteed a club a player's service for as long it wished.

The American Association. A rival league, the American Association, was formed in 1882. Cincinnati was its champion that year, while Chicago was the champion of the National League. At the end of the season, the teams met for the first-ever World Series. Only two games were played, with each team winning one.

The American League. The American Association lasted only eight years. It folded in 1891, in the same year that the American League began operation. The American League (which had previously been known as the Western League) proved to be as tough as the National League. From 1903 to the present, the champs of the two leagues (National and American) have met in the World Series. In 1969, each league was split into two divisions, and a League Championship Series was created to determine the pennant winners—and who would go to the World Series.

The Negro Leagues. The first all-black pro team was the 1885 Cuban Giants. By the 1920s, there were many such teams, and they organized into "Negro Leagues." Major leaguers sometimes played against them in postseason games. They soon discovered that the black teams were just as good as the all-white ones.

Jackie Robinson was the first African American to play on an otherwise all-white major league team. In 1947, he stepped onto the field in a Brooklyn Dodgers' uniform. That year he batted .297, led the league in stolen bases, and was voted Rookie of the Year. Most important, he led the way in bringing an end to segregation in sports.

A League for Ladies. In 1943, many ballplayers were off fighting in World War II. Chicago Cubs' owner, P. Wrigley, organized a pro softball league for women. The idea was to offer fans pretty faces and good baseball, which quickly proved to be a winning combination. The following year, the All-American Girls Baseball League stopped playing *softball*—and began playing *hardball* instead. The league lasted until 1954.

Did You Know?

In 1922, during a double-header, two players from one of the teams were traded to the opposing team between games!

Girls play hardball!

Baseball Equipment

Some of the most interesting changes in baseball involved the equipment.

The Ball. Originally, the major leagues used a ball with a rubber center. In 1909, the center was changed to cork enclosed in rubber and tightly wound with layers of cotton and wool yarn. In one ball, there are 150 yards (137.2 m) of cotton yarn and 219 yards (200.3 m) of wool yarn!

Bats. Early on in baseball, players sometimes used huge bats. Some of these looked like war clubs, others like big, flat paddles. In 1859, the superhuge bats were outlawed. Today's major-league bats can be no more than 42 inches (1.1 m) long and 2-3/4 inches (7 cm) in diameter, and they must be made of wood. Aluminum bats are used at every level of the game—except the major leagues.

Gloves. Ouuuch! Baseball gloves were not invented until 1875. Made of leather, early gloves were small, and didn't have padding, or laces connecting the fingers. The first ones were for catchers. After a while, players at other positions began wearing gloves, too.

Catcher's Gear. Fred Thayer, a baseball enthusiast, invented the catcher's mask in 1875. He made it from an old wire-mesh mask of the kind worn by fencers (sword fighters). The catcher's mask of today has a flap hanging from it to protect the throat. The flap was first used by catcher Steve Yeager of the Dodgers in 1977. Earlier that year while catching a game, a bat shattered, and Yeager was stabbed in the throat by a large, flying splinter of wood. He had the throat protector made to order; soon, other pro catchers were following his example.

Chest protectors were invented in the same year as catchers' masks, in 1875. At first, pro catchers thought the things made them look like sissies, and they refused to wear them. But after ten more years of getting battered by fastballs, they finally started strapping them on. By 1908, they were strapping on shin guards, as well.

Helmets. In 1952, the Pittsburgh Pirates introduced plastic baseball helmets. The players had to wear them all the time, even when they were on defense. After a few years, it was decided that players only needed to wear helmets when they were batting. The early batting helmet had no earflap. The earflap was developed in Little League play and copied by the major leagues.

Did You Know? In 1931, Joe Sprinz of the Cleveland Indians caught a baseball dropped 800 feet (243.8 m) from a hovering blimp. The impact created a shockwave through his body that fractured his jaw!

On the Move!

For the first 77 years of its existence, Major League Baseball was very stable. The teams stayed put; not since the emergence of the National League in 1858, had a team moved. But then in 1953, the Boston Braves became the Milwaukee Braves. In 1966, they moved again—and became the Atlanta Braves.

In 1954, the St. Louis Browns moved east to Maryland and became the Baltimore Orioles.

In 1955, the Philadelphia Athletics became the Kansas City Athletics. In 1968, they moved again and became the Oakland Athletics, or A's, as they are sometimes called.

In 1958, pro baseball spread to the West Coast. The Brooklyn Dodgers set up shop in Los Angeles. The New York Giants relocated to San Francisco.

Baseball Firsts

In 1998, Mark McGwire became the first baseball player to hit 70 home runs in a season. The first night game in the majors was played on May 23, 1935. Heavily padded gloves for catchers were worn for the first time during the 1891 season. Baseball "firsts" such as these have always been a fascinating part of the game's history and lore. Here are some other ones:

◆ 1845—J.W. Davis is fined 6¢ for swearing at an umpire, the first fine in baseball history.

◆ 1860—The New York Gothams make baseball's first "road trip."

◆ 1875—Joe Borden of the Philadelphia Athletics pitches baseball's first no-hitter.

◆ 1882—Catcher Deacon White of the Cincinnati Red Stockings becomes the first player to wear sunglasses while playing.

◆ 1908—The first electronic scoreboard is used. Also, baseball cards are first introduced.

◆ 1916—The Chicago Cubs decide to let fans keep balls hit into the stands. (Twenty-five years would pass before all clubs adopted this policy.)

◆ 1921—The first radio broadcast of a major-league game is aired on KDKA radio in Pittsburgh. The game was between the Pittsburgh Pirates and the Philadelphia Phillies.

◆ 1930—The American League makes numbers on uniforms mandatory for all teams.

◆ 1931—Playing for the Memphis Lookouts in an exhibition game against the New York Yankees, Jackie Mitchell becomes the first woman to pitch against major-league players. In the game, she strikes out both Babe Ruth and Lou Gehrig.

◆ 1933—To spark interest in baseball, it was decided to pit the most outstanding players from the American League against those from the National League. In 1933, the first All-Star Game was played in Chicago, with the American League winning 4—2.

◆ 1934—The Cincinnati Reds become the first team to travel by airplane to a game. (In 1946, the New York Yankees became the first team to travel by plane the entire season.)

◆ 1935—The Cincinnati Reds host the Philadelphia Phillies in the first major-league night game. (Minor-league and amateur teams had been playing under the lights on a regular basis for more than a decade.)

◆ 1939—The Brooklyn Dodgers meet the Cincinnati Reds in the first televised game. Also, Little League baseball plays its first official season.

The year: 1939. Kids get to see baseball on TV for the first time!

◆ 1947—The Little League World Series is held for the first time, in Williamsport, Pennsylvania.

◆ 1960—Players' names begin appearing on uniforms.

◆ 1992—The Toronto Blue Jays become the first non-U.S. team to win the World Series.

◆ 2004—The Boston Red Sox become the first team to come back from a 0—3 deficit to win the World Series

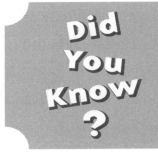

Did You Know ?

On the average, it takes eight hours to clean up the stands after a major-league ball game.

Traditions

In 1910, when President Taft threw out the opening-day pitch for a major-league game, it was a first. It also happened to become a tradition, a custom that would be repeated every year.

Another baseball tradition is the playing of "The Star-Spangled Banner" before a game. It began during the 1917 baseball season while the United States was fighting in World War I. As a show of patriotism, before each game, everyone in the stadium sang the national anthem.

Surprisingly, we've been singing "Take Me out to the Ball Game" even longer than "The Star-Spangled Banner." In 1908, singer and songwriter Jack Norworth wrote "Take Me out to the Ball Game"—which is now sung during another tradition, the "seventh-inning stretch." (Incredibly, Norworth did not see his first baseball game till 34 years later, in 1942! He loved to write songs but didn't give a hoot about baseball!)

The Doubleday Myth

Abner Doubleday did not invent baseball.

He grew up in Cooperstown, New York. As a kid, he played baseball. He was a courageous general in the Union army. And he was a talented writer.

But he had nothing to do with the invention of baseball.

Here's why so many people think he did:

In 1907, a special baseball commission was appointed "to determine the origins of 'the great American pastime.'" Right off, the commission set out to prove that baseball was an entirely American creation, and in no way related to the English game of "rounders." After two long years of research, the members of the commission found nothing to back up this claim.

But then one day, they received a letter from an old man named Graves, who had been one of Abner Doubleday's boyhood buddies back in Cooperstown, New York. In shaky handwriting, Graves wrote that Doubleday, entirely on his own, had invented baseball.

Graves had no proof. None. But his letter was just the thing the commission had been hoping for, and was just what they wanted to hear: A bright, clever, and respectable all-American man had invented baseball all on his own. Graves did not mean any harm. But the old man was wrong, if only for one reason—baseball had already been invented when Doubleday was born.

Actually, if one man is to get credit for inventing the modern game of baseball, it should be Alexander Cartwright. In 1845, he headed a special committee whose job it was to standardize the game.

The first thing Cartwright did was to create the diamond-shaped playing field of today. He eliminated fourth base. To score, a runner had to get back to where he started—home plate.

Cartwright and his committee also rewrote the rules. They made three strikes (instead of four) an out. The players also had to bat in turn, in a specific order, and after three outs, players changed sides—from offense to defense. The number of players on each team would be 9, not 12, as it had been originally. Last, and certainly not least, Cartwright came up with the idea of innings—nine of them, as today.

In 1939, the Baseball Hall of Fame was built in Cooperstown, New York, Abner Doubleday's hometown. There, you will find bats used by sluggers like Babe Ruth, gloves worn by magnificent fielders such as Ozzie Smith, and balls thrown in treacherous curves by pitchers such as Sandy Koufax. Truly, the Cooperstown Hall of Fame is a great place to visit. But if anybody tells you that Doubleday invented baseball—and Cooperstown is where he did it—maybe you can politely set them straight: Alexander Cartwright, not Abner Doubleday, deserves the credit for creating pro baseball—and making it the game it is today.

And don't forget one other thing—though Cartwright greatly improved the game, he did not invent it. Kids did! And they did not do it for money. They did it just for fun!

Did You Know?

In August 1971, the Pittsburgh Pirates became the first pro team to field nine players who were either African-American or Latino. Coincidentally, they won the World Series that year.

PRO BASKETBALL

Naismithball

James Naismith, a Canadian-born American, invented modern basketball. Here's how it happened:

In 1891, Naismith was a teacher at a boys' school, the Springfield, Massachusetts, YMCA (Young Men's Christian Association) Training School. In the fall, the students were outside playing what was then a new game—football. In the spring, they played baseball. But during the cold winter months in Massachusetts, the boys were stuck indoors, down in the school's basement gymnasium.

There were only three things for the guys to do. First, there were body exercises. But the thrill of doing push-ups, sit-ups, and jumping jacks wore off pretty quickly. Gymnastics were better, but even they got old after a while. Then there was marching! Believe it or not, marching was another indoor activity. With the gym teachers leading the way, the guys would march around the gym like a bunch of soldiers.

For a long time, the teachers had been trying to come up with a new sport that students could play in the gym. So far, they hadn't come up with a single decent idea.

James Naismith, the newest and youngest of the

Dr. James Naismith

gym teachers, was determined to figure something out. One day after school, in December 1891, he went down to the gym. He looked around the empty place, trying to think of a game that could be played there. His first idea was some kind of indoor football. Instead of goal posts, he decided a wooden box would be nailed to the balcony at either end of the gym. The kids would pass the football to their teammates and then one would take the ball and try to get it into the box.

One problem: no boxes.

"But I do have two peach baskets," the janitor told Naismith.

The men nailed those to the balcony, one at each end of the gym. It just so happened that the balcony was ten feet (3.1 m) above the floor—and for that reason, that is the height of a basketball hoop to this very day.

Naismith took shot after shot with a football. Because of its egglike shape, the football bounced around crazily, going everywhere but in. Naismith spotted a soccer ball. He took a few shots, and finally made the first basket ever!

That night, he wrote down rules for the new game.

The next day, his class filed into the gym. Coach Naismith read the rules aloud and explained how his new game was played. Since there were 18 boys in the class, Naismith made two teams of nine.

For that reason, for the first few years of the game, the official number of players on each team was nine. Later, the number was reduced to seven. It eased up to eight, then finally, in 1897, plunged to five, where it remains today.

Naismith's students loved the game. *Naismithball*. That's what they called it. And it would still be called that, except for one person: James Naismith. "No, gentlemen," he said, "I prefer that it be called basketball."

High school basketball in 1899

Basketball Takes Off!

In addition to inventing and naming the sport almost single-handedly, James Naismith popularized basketball. In 1892, shortly after his students returned from Christmas vacation, he organized the first game between two schools. On an icy day in February of 1892, two local YMCA schools—Central and Armory Hill—played each other. Hard to believe, but the final score of the game was a 2—2 tie! In a rematch a month later, Armory Hill won by a whopping 1—0! Within a few years after its invention, there were YMCA basketball teams all over the New England area.

A Girls Game, Too!

Naismith soon had girls in on the action. In March of 1892, the first-ever all-female game was played. The game was between a team of female teachers and female students. One of the players on the teachers' team, Maude Sherman, was very pretty and a super player. Mr. Naismith and Ms. Sherman fell in love, and soon were married.

Girls playing basketball —December 1926.

Most people don't know it, but college basketball was first played by women, not men. In 1892, Vassar and Smith, both women's colleges, added basketball to their athletic programs. Later the same year, Vanderbilt became the first men's college to play the game.

Going Pro

Basketball went pro a lot sooner than you might think—in 1896, only five years after it was invented.

Despite the low scores, basketball was a really rough and wild game in the early days. The action did not even stop when a ball went out of bounds. Chairs went flying and people got knocked flat as the players fought each other—*and the fans*—for the ball.

Believing the game to be too rough, many YMCA leaders wanted to see an end to basketball; they refused to let teams play in YMCA gyms. As a result, many YMCA players had to take the action elsewhere. The teams played in dance halls, armories, barns, and roller-skating rinks. In order to rent the places, admission was charged, usually 25¢ a person. Each player was paid $15, with the captains each receiving a $1 bonus.

Pro basketball was born.

Did You Know? James Naismith passed away in 1939. He lived long enough to see his invention become one of the most popular sports in the country, and to see the first 43 years of the professional game.

Caged Cagers

Early pro games were rowdy affairs. As in hockey games today, there were many fistfights; sometimes the fans would even get in on the action! Another problem—when a ball went up in the stands, the fans would often keep it. To remedy this, the playing area was enclosed with chicken wire or other see-through fencing. The fencing kept the ball in play and the fans out. It was like a cage, and pro players were called "cagers" back then.

Other Strange Courts

In 1928, two pro teams played in the weirdest arena in the history of pro ball—an indoor swimming pool that had been drained for the winter! As players headed toward the basket in the deep end, they were going downhill; as they headed the other way, toward the shallow end, they were running uphill.

Another strange court was one used in 1903. It was in a basement of a building, and there were steam pipes all along the walls. The pipes hissed out hot steam at the players. And when the players went out of bounds, frequently they crashed into the superheated pipes. All the players went home with burns.

In the same year, a game was played on a court with a potbellied stove in the middle! Another was played with the baskets hidden by boilers. The players had to shoot over the boilers when trying to make a basket!

Having a potbellied stove in the middle of the floor was unique. But it was *not* unusual for there to be a pillar or post in the middle of the court. Its purpose was to support the roof. But pro players put it to another use—and in the process created a new type of play. When an offensive player ran his defender into a post, he was using what was called the "post" play. This term is still used today. It refers to the center using his body to block opponents from a teammate. By doing this, he gives his teammate a good, clear shot at the basket.

Uniforms

In the first few years of the game, amateur players wore long pants with long-sleeved jerseys. By the time basketball became a pro sport, the players wore sleeveless jerseys fashioned after upper-body underwear. They wore short pants called knickers and long stockings. On their feet, they wore soft leather shoes—until 1906, when rubber basketball shoes were invented.

Bring Your Own Basket!

The pro teams played wherever there was money. They had to bring their own ball, and they often had to bring their own baskets, too!

The equipment had to be portable, something the players could lug from place to place. Usually this meant using a basket without a backboard, one consisting of a pole with a basket on top. Barney Sedran, a 5' 4" (1.6 m) guard, holds the pro record for the most baskets made in a game using such a basket: 17.

The first pro backboards were made of wire mesh, which was chosen because it enabled the fans behind the boards to see the action. In 1908, transparent backboards of extremely durable glass were invented. The pros began using them right away, in 1909. But not until the 1946—47 season did the colleges allow their use.

Did You Know? In the 1940s, Hank Luisetti invented the one-handed shot by accident. He did not have the upper-body strength to shoot two-handed, the way everybody else did.

Trash-Can Ball to Bag Ball

One of the biggest problems with early basketball, both for the amatuer players as well as the pros, was the basket itself. The first baskets, peach baskets, weren't very durable. They got smashed up and fell apart too fast, as did woven baskets, which were given a shot for a while. Strange but true—the first thing to be taken out of basketball was the basket!

In place of baskets, trash cans—either metal or wire mesh—were used. One problem with the cans was that a shot could be perfect, but because of the hard sides and bottoms, the ball would bounce right back out. To keep this from happening, the pros began using net bags of heavy cord hanging from metal hoops.

Incredibly, for the first five years of the game, the bottom was left in the "basket." Every time a shot was made, someone had to climb a ladder to get the ball out! There was one exception, however. Sometimes a small hole was made in the bottom of the net bag. The hole was there so that the ball could be knocked back out using a long stick.

Getting the ball out, either with a ladder or a pole, soon became the most boring and annoying part of the game—for the players and spectators alike. Clearly, a change was needed. In 1895, manufacturers of sporting goods claimed to have solved the big how-to-get-the-ball-out problem. Their solution was rather interesting, to say the least (and silly, to tell the truth). The company made a basketball basket that was sort of like a toilet. From the basket, ten feet up, dangled a long pull-down chain. The chain opened the bottom of the basket and let the ball out.

The obvious was still being missed.

Finally, one day in 1896, someone figured out the simple solution. The man's name was never written down for the history books. All that is known about him is that he was a semi-pro player who lived in Detroit. The man went and got a pair of scissors. Then he climbed a stepladder and proceeded to cut the bottom out of the net.

Scoring

Why were the scores so low in the first years of basketball?

One reason is that until 1893, a field goal or "basket" counted as only one point. In 1894, the value of a field goal shot up to three points. In 1896, the pros changed a field goal from three to two points, and the amateurs followed their example. In 1961, the pros re-introduced the three-point shot, but only for extra long shots, the length of which has varied from 22 feet (6.7 m) from the basket to 25 feet (7.6 m); the colleges adopted the three-point rule in 1986, but the length of the shot needed to be only 19 feet, 9 inches (6 m).

Today, scoring has skyrocketed; pro teams routinely score more than a hundred points in a game. Scores from the early days—scores such as 4—3—sound ridiculous. But that's the way it was.

Foul Stuff

Under Naismith's original rules, there was no such thing as a free throw. Instead, a team was awarded one point if the opposing team committed a three-rules violation. The violations had to be consecutive. That is, one team had to be guilty of three fouls in a row—with no fouls being committed in the meantime by the other team.

The free throw was not invented until basketball's third year, 1893. Originally, the free-throw line was 20 feet (6.1 m) from the basket (instead of 15 feet [4.6 m], as today). Only one shot was taken; if made, it counted as three points. Especially in the pros, the person taking the shot usually was not the person fouled. Instead, each team had its own specialist free-throw shooter (which sometimes was the coach!). Finally, in 1923, the pros did away with the free-throw specialist; the player who was fouled had to go to the line himself and take the free throw.

No Dribbling Allowed

In Naismith's amateur version of the game, the ball could be advanced only by passing it.

When players went pro, they soon began changing the rules. They began dribbling. It might sound crazy, but at first they dribbled overhead, tapping the ball up in the air as they ran!

It wasn't long before they realized how ridiculous this was.

Pro rules allowed for players to bounce the ball on the ground as many times as they wanted. Taking advantage of this rule, players started running at the same time they bounced the ball. Dribbling had begun!

Dutch Wolfarth, a pro player in the first years of the game, was considered a sensation. Wolfarth, playing for the Philadelphia Jaspers, amazed spectators by dribbling without looking at the ball. (This is something many ten-year-old kids today do all the time!)

The First Pro League

The first pro league, the National Basketball League, was formed in 1898. There were six teams, and all were from the Philadelphia area. The league lasted only two years before disbanding.

The first pro team to make any real money was the Buffalo Germans.

They started out in 1895 as an unpaid YMCA team made up of 14-year-old boys. By the time the players were 17 and 18 years-old, they had formed a pro team. Over the next 20 years, the Germans had a 792—86 record, including a 111-game winning streak! Because of their popularity, the team made as much as $500 for playing a three-game series, which was a lot of money at the time.

Other basketball leagues began forming. The Central League lasted from 1906 to 1912, the Eastern League from 1909 to 1923. Two other leagues from this period were the New York State League and the Tri-County League.

Some of today's basketball fans are bothered by the fact that players frequently move from one team to another. One season, a player is playing for "their" team but the next season, he's playing for a rival team.

However, things were even worse in the early years of the game. Players switched teams from game to game. Very simply, they played for whatever league and team would pay them the most on a given night.

During this era, a pro team known as the New York Trojans added two new elements to the game. The first of these was the bounce pass (tossing the ball to a teammate on one bounce). The other was the "fast break." In those days, there was a center jump after every basket that was made. The Trojans' version of the fast break was for the entire team to race downcourt together if the center jump went their way. Today, the term refers not only to the center jump, but to anytime team members *break* loose as a unit and run together as *fast* as they can to get a basket.

The Original Celtics (1920–1931)

The "Original Celtics" were the first really powerful team in pro basketball. The team was from New York, and is in no way related to the modern Boston Celtics.

Though New York City was the Original Celtics' base of operations, the team was primarily a traveling one. When the players weren't playing in New York, they "barnstormed," which means they played local teams in various cities. There were six paid players on the team. The coach, Johnny Witty, played when needed.

The Original Celtics beat just about anybody they played. This included teams from the ABL, the newly formed American Basketball League. In 1926, the Original Celtics joined the ABL and easily won the league's first two championships. Because they were so good, the team was broken up and its talented players spread among other teams. This created competitive balance by making the teams in the League more equal. But fans missed seeing "the Celts," and the ABL folded in 1931.

Did You Know? In the 1961-62 season, Wilt Chamberlain averaged 50 points a game, and in one game he scored 100 points (the only pro to ever do so).

The Ballroom Rens (1922–1940)

During the 1920s and 1930s, there were professional "hotel" teams. Hotel teams usually played at night, right on the ballroom floor of a hotel. Sometimes the basketball action was during an intermission in the dancing; sometimes it was a special event that completely took the place of everything else.

The first really great hotel team was the Rens. This all-black team got its name from where it played—at the Renaissance Casino Ballroom in Harlem. Because they were the best, a ticket to see the Rens cost more than a ticket to see any of the hotel teams in New York. Admission was $1, 25¢ above the usual price.

The Rens were the only team of the era that were as good as the Original Celtics. In the 1926-27 season, these two great teams met for a six-game series. But to the fans' disappointment, nothing was decided as far as which team was best. The Celtics and the Rens split the series, with each team winning three games.

The Harlem Globetrotters (1927–)

The Globetrotters have always been full of surprises, and that includes their history. They began as a serious hotel team. Playing for the Savoy hotel in Chicago, they were known as the "Savoy Big Five."

Their founder and first coach was Abe Saperstein. Saperstein was a roly-poly, 5' 3" (1.6 m) guard. After playing for two years at the University of Illinois, he began coaching the Savoy Big Five. When the owner of the hotel complained that the all-black team was not attracting enough customers, Saperstein changed the team's name to the Harlem Globetrotters. "We chose Harlem," said Saperstein, "because Harlem was to our black players what Jerusalem was to [a Jewish person such as] me. As for Globetrotters, well, we had dreams. We hoped to travel."

Today, the Globetrotters travel in two custom-built buses in which the seats are spaced far enough apart to give the long-legged players room to stretch out and nap as they travel from city to city. However, they didn't travel in such luxury in the beginning.

On January 7, 1927, the Trotters traveled to their first road game outside of Chicago. The entire team of five players stuffed themselves into Saperstein's Model T Ford for a trip to Hinckley, Illinois. Their $75 fee was split seven ways—with one share to each player, and two shares to coach and promoter Saperstein.

Harlem Globetrotter
Meadowlark Lemon kicks a basket!

For their first 20 years, the Globetrotters were a serious basketball team, not a show. But as they toured night after night, they became tired of simply beating the other team; they started adding some fancy ballhandling and clowning around into the games. The Globetrotters became even more of a draw, as fans came out in droves to see the team's wild antics.

The NBL . . . & the Trotters

During the time that the Trotters were getting together, a new, more high-powered league was formed, the National Basketball League. The NBL, formed in 1937, consisted of teams in several Midwestern cities, including Fort Wayne, Indiana; Akron, Ohio; and Oshkosh, Wisconsin. Later, several other teams joined the NBL.

One of these teams would, for a time, be known as the Minneapolis Lakers. In 1948, the Minneapolis Lakers won the NBL championship. Afterwards, Abe Saperstein arranged for a game to be played between the Lakers and the Globetrotters. The Trotters stunned the basketball world by winning 61—59.

Having beaten the champions of "ordinary" basketball, the Globetrotters started performing more and more wacky tricks and crazy stunts to please their ever-growing number of fans. They called these stunts "reems." One of the players, Inman Jackson, would roll the ball up one arm, across the back of his shoulders, and down the other arm. "Babe" Pressley would throw the ball across the court with so much backspin that it would bounce right back to him—as though it were on the end of a string. Over the years, different players have come and gone. Goose Tatum, Curly Neal, and Meadowlark Lemon all have added their comic genius to the game.

Did You Know?

For the first 41 years of their existence, the Harlem Globetrotters did not play any games in Harlem. They did not make their first appearance there until 1968.

The NBA

In 1946, the Basketball Association of America was formed. At first the BAA was a rival to the NBL (National Basketball League). In 1948, the two merged and became today's NBA (National Basketball Association). Over the years, the NBA has adopted many of the rules that continue to be used in the game of basketball today.

In 1950, the Fort Wayne Pistons beat the Lakers 19—18. Mostly, the Pistons just held the ball and played keep-away, often for many minutes at a time. To eliminate such boring farces, the NBA adopted a rule in which each team had to take a shot within 24 seconds after receiving the ball. This made the games exciting; it kept the players shooting instead of passing the ball around for an eternity.

The NBA has become one of the most successful professional sports organizations in history. One reason is that the rules changes are always directed at making basketball a faster, more exciting game. For example, the 24-second clock makes the game move at a very fast pace. The free-substitution rule means that players can come into or out

Kareem Abdul-Jabbar goes "flying" on a sky-hook.

of the game as often as desired, which results in always having fresh players on the court. The three-point shot adds a whole new dimension, since a team that is two points behind can take the lead on the basis of a single shot. Most important of all, though, is the consistently high skill level of the players. Try to imagine what the NBA would be like if there had never been a Wilt Chamberlain. Or, how about Bill Russell, Larry Bird, Magic Johnson, Kareem Abdul-Jabbar, Michael Jordan, Shaquille O'Neal, Tim Duncan, or Josh Kidd?

Did You Know?

Michael Jordan was paid a 30-million-dollar salary for playing the 1996–97 season for the Chicago Bulls.

Women Go Pro

From the earliest days of the game, females have been playing basketball. However, almost a century passed before women started playing pro ball.

In 1986, Nancy Lieberman-Cline became the first woman to play in a *men's* professional league. She played for the Springfield Fame. Another standout was Lynette Woodward, who played for the Harlem Globetrotters for two seasons, 1985–1987.

Women finally got their own league ten years later, in 1996, when the Women's American Basketball League was formed. The next season, 1997, saw the creation of the WNBA, the Women's National Basketball Association. The WNBA was started and first sponsored by the NBA, and each of the teams is owned and operated by the NBA team in that city. The women play

At left, Sheryl Swoopes—in for a layup.

in NBA arenas, although in some cases the seating is modified to create a smaller, more intimate setting. Lisa Leslie, Rebecca Lobo, and Sheryl Swoopes were the first three players signed by the WNBA.

Pro Basketball—Past & Future

The history of pro basketball is an incredible story. And you've only heard part of it. You did not read about when—and why—the slam dunk was once illegal. Also not included is the story of "company teams," and how for a time the major U.S. corporations all had pro and semipro teams. And there is one very interesting but unpleasant story—that of basketball's 1951 point-fixing scandal.

Basketball's past is fascinating.

So is its future. There are presently all sorts of changes that have been proposed. Some say that the court should be larger to provide more room for today's bigger players. Another recommendation is that the number of players on a team be reduced to four. The most popular suggestion is that the basket, because the players are so tall, should be raised from where it has been for over a century, from 10 feet to 12 (3.1 m to 3.7).

What the future holds for pro basketball is going to be extremely interesting to see—probably as interesting as its past.

Did You Know?

Gheorge Muresan, at 7' 7" (2.3 m), is the tallest player in NBA history.

PRO FOOTBALL

Roman Football

The first pro football players were soldiers in ancient Rome, in 1 A.D. Their salary was paid in salt! The salt was used to trade for other goods.

The game these soldiers played had 34 men on a team, and it was very rough! You see, the purpose of this Roman version of football was to toughen up soldiers for battle. But there was one problem. So many soldiers got beaten up and broken up in games that they were no longer able to fight in battle! For this reason, the game was banned.

England, 1938: Teams from two schools go at it in a rugby match.

The Bloody English Game

In England, football was also first played by soldiers. Legend has it that in the eighth century, a gory custom started there. If the English won a battle, they chopped off the head of the leader of the losing army. Then, "for fun," they'd kick the head around with their feet.

But there wasn't a battle everyday, so the English soldiers took to drying the bladders of cows and goats, and then inflating them. To make these "bladder balls" stronger, they covered them with pigskin. (That is why, to this day, the inside of a football is called the "bladder" and the ball itself a "pigskin.")

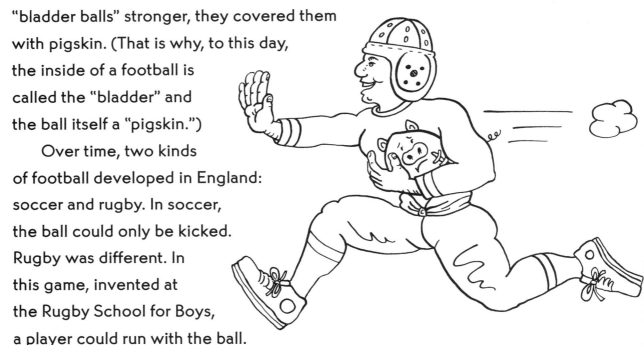

Over time, two kinds of football developed in England: soccer and rugby. In soccer, the ball could only be kicked. Rugby was different. In this game, invented at the Rugby School for Boys, a player could run with the ball.

American Football!

Football reached America in the early 1800s. At first, it was a combination of rugby and soccer, with the rules of play constantly changing. Little by little, a uniquely American game began to emerge. The game consisted mostly of running, blocking, and tackling. As in rugby, players ran with the ball and they could pass it backwards or laterally (to the side), but not forward. Crossing the goal line with the ball was usually worth one point, while kicking it across was worth as much as four points.

Simply kicking the ball over the goal line became too easy. To make kicking a goal harder, a narrow space in the middle of the goal line was added. The ball had to be kicked into this area in order to score. Later, goal posts marked the area, and finally, in the early 1880s, a crossbar was placed between the posts.

At first, football was only played by college teams or by what were called "town teams." On Saturdays, the colleges played. On Sundays, the players from two towns would meet for a game.

Town Teams and Pro Ball

Professional football was born on an ordinary Sunday in 1895. Two town teams in Pennsylvania met for a game, and for the first time, charged admission so that the players could make a little money. Each player received $10.

By the early 1900s, with increased competition between town teams, players were being paid as much as $600 a game. Some of the best players around were college kids. These college players often played for their schools on Saturdays and for professional town teams on Sundays.

The First Pro Teams

The Chicago Cardinals. The Cardinals are the oldest pro team still in existence today. In 1899, the year the team was founded, it was called the Morgan Athletic Club. By 1920, the name had been changed to the Chicago Cardinals. In that year, the team challenged Chicago's other pay-for-play team, the Tigers, to a game. The stakes were high—the losing team had to get out of town! The Cardinals won a bitter, bruising contest by a score of 6—3. The Tigers, heads hanging, hit the road.

The Bears Come to Town. The Cardinals did not have long to celebrate being the only team in Chicago. One year later, in 1921, player-owner George Halas brought the Decatur Staleys football team to the city. He changed the name to the Bears and set up shop in Wrigley Field.

In their first meeting, the Cardinals tore up the Bears. They also took on and beat teams from other Midwestern and Eastern cities on a regular basis.

Chicago Bears on the bench in 1925

But in 1928, their fortunes changed for the worse. That year, the Cardinals won only one of seven games. In 1938, they won only two of eleven games.

Soon, the Bears ruled the city. Their nickname became "Monsters of the Midway." As for the Cardinals, their days in Chicago were numbered.

The Philadelphia Athletics. In 1902, a man by the name of Connie Mack organized the Philadelphia Athletics football team. After a winning season, a showdown game was arranged against a tough Pittsburgh squad. The Athletics won the game, 6—3. For this feat, they claimed the "Professional Football Championship of America." The Athletics also played in the first night football game. Under the lights in Elmira, New York, they crushed the Kanaweola Athletic Club.

Green Bay Packers. In August 1919, several men met in the office of the local newspaper in Green Bay, Wisconsin. They discussed forming a football team. The owners of the Indian Packing Company said they would put up a little money. They also agreed to buy most of the equipment and allow use of the company's athletic field.

Shortly, the name of the company was changed to Acme Packing. As for the new team, they called themselves the Packers.

The Packers played against other teams from Wisconsin and Upper Michigan. Games were played in an open field with no fences or bleachers. No admission fee was charged. Instead, the fans "passed the hat" (made donations). Whatever money was collected was divided equally among the players. The Packers won ten games their first season and lost only one.

Did You Know?

In a 1940 title game, the Chicago Bears showed up wearing low-cut shoes, a big change from the traditional black high tops.

43

Pro Football Gets Organized

The APFA. In 1920, owners of several pro teams got together at the Hupmobile Car Agency in Canton, Ohio. After a lot of talking and squabbling, they decided to create the APFA, the American Professional Football Association.

There were 11 teams in the APFA. Among them were the Akron Steels, Buffalo All-Americans, Chicago Cardinals, Canton Bulldogs, Cleveland Panthers, and Detroit Heralds. The admission fee to become a part of the new association was $100 per team.

OOPS! The organizers made a huge mistake. It may be hard to believe, but they did not plan a schedule of games! Teams more or less played when they felt like it.

Early face mask and helmet

Some teams hardly played at all—and soon dropped out altogether. The association folded at the end of the season.

The NFL. Two years later, in 1922, the owners took another shot at getting organized. This time they succeeded. Eighteen teams joined what the owners decided to call the National Football League.

However, a scandal that same year almost destroyed the NFL. It was discovered that the Green Bay Packers were breaking one of the basic rules of the league. Incredibly, they were using some of the country's best high school players on their team, which was not allowed. The kids had been given phony names to hide their identity, and sent in to play.

The kids were sent back where they belonged—to school. The Packers were fined. The NFL survived the scandal.

A decade later, the NFL was stronger than ever. In the early 1930s, it was agreed that the NFL would split into two divisions. The winning team from each division would meet at the end of the regular season for a championship game.

The Equipment

The NFL was born in the 1920s. Back then, teams gave the players a jersey and socks, and that's all! Players had to provide the rest of their uniform. Most used what they had worn when they played in college, from helmets and shoes to shoulder pads and pants. To say the least, the players on a team were a ragtag, mismatched looking bunch.

Helmets. In the 1920s, most players wore soft leather helmets. The helmets were so pliable they could be folded up and shoved into a pocket. Some players wore nothing to protect their heads except long hair tied up into a bun.

A few players wore "nose-protector" helmets. These

45

A Rams' helmet

first-ever face guards were pretty worthless. Most players in those days had at least a few missing teeth. Some had hardly any teeth at all!

The helmet of the 1930s was a hard-leather version with a molded crown and reinforced fiber shell. John Riddell developed a plastic helmet that was first used in 1939, but it did not catch on until after World War II. One reason is that these early plastic helmets often cracked and fell apart. They were banned in 1948. But then manufacturers invented a stronger plastic model, and the ban was lifted in 1949.

Over the years, there had been many attempts to make a good face mask. But all were flops. Finally, in 1955, a face guard that worked was invented—one that consisted of a curved steel bar. Soon, the single bar was doubled, then tripled. Eventually, this became the "bird cage" worn by modern players.

In 1956, the Cleveland Browns rigged up a sound receiver inside the quarterback's helmet. The idea was for the coach to call the play from the sidelines by speaking into a microphone. The gadget soon ran into a big problem, however. Outside interference made hearing the coach very difficult. In one game, the Cleveland quarterback threw off his helmet in disgust. "I'm getting people calling for taxis!" The device was banned by year's end. It did not reappear for 30 years.

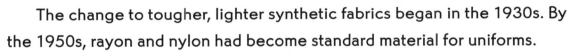

Uniforms. In the first years of pro football, pants were made of heavy brown canvas. The jerseys were made of wool, and looked more like sweaters. When it rained, the uniforms would absorb so much water that they could double in weight!

The change to tougher, lighter synthetic fabrics began in the 1930s. By the 1950s, rayon and nylon had become standard material for uniforms.

The first shoulder pads were made of wool-lined leather. Cup-shaped pads protected the shoulders. And these were connected to a vestlike leather garment to protect the chest and upper back.

The shoes worn in football's early days were leather high-tops. The cleats were made of tapered, hardened leather nailed to the sole of the shoe. Helmetmaker John Riddell came up with a clever idea for a better type of cleats. Made of iron, they were detachable. When the weather was good, players needed short cleats. But when it was bad, they needed longer cleats to get better footing in the snow and mud. For bad-weather days, the short cleats could be removed and long ones bolted on instead. Detachable cleats soon became popular—and are still used today.

The Tee. During a game in 1919, a player by the name of Ada Bowser realized he could get more distance on his kicks if the ball was raised off the ground a bit. He mixed up some mud in an old washtub. Before each kick he would get a couple of handfuls of mud, then plop them on the ground and form a little hill. Presto! He had invented what eventually became known as the "kicking tee."

Ball. One of the biggest problems in football's early days was the ball itself. It was fat and heavy, and consisted of a rubber bladder stuck in a leather casing, with no lining between the leather and rubber. The more the ball got beaten around in a game, the fatter and more hard-to-handle it got. A famous player by the name of Ernie Nevers, in an early 1920s game, punted a ball that exploded on impact! George Halas, fielding a kickoff, once found only a totally deflated, shredded slab of leather landing in his hands! In 1925, equipment manufacturers designed a new, sturdily lined football. From then on, the ball stayed in shape!

In the 1930s, rubber footballs were given a try. In the late 1950s and early 1960s, teams used white balls in night games because they were easier to see in the dark. Neither of these experiments lasted very long. Quarterbacks found rubber balls harder to throw; receivers complained that white footballs were difficult to see against the bright lights used for night games.

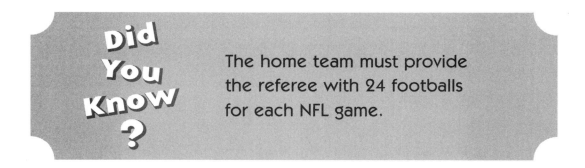

Did You Know?

The home team must provide the referee with 24 footballs for each NFL game.

Scoring

In 1897, a touchdown was worth five points. The goal kick made after a touchdown was worth one point as it is today. A field goal was worth five points. Tackling a player in his own end zone for a "safety" was worth two points.

Throughout the years, point values changed to those of today. In 1904, the value of a field goal was reduced to four points. By 1909, it had been reduced to three points, as it is now. A few years later, in 1912, the value of a touchdown was increased from five to six points. In 1960, the new AFL (American Football League) introduced the idea of having the option of a two-point conversion.

Nutty Old Rules!

Playing on the Edge. In the early 1920s, if a player was tackled near the sideline, that's where the next play began. The team had to waste a play just trying to get back to the middle of the field, into operating territory. Not until 1933 was a "side zone" of ten yards (9.1 m) created. This meant that the ball was brought a minimum of ten yards toward the center of the field.

Passing. The forward pass became legal in 1906. But well into the 1920s, there were some strange rules on the books. The passer had to be five yards (4.6 m) behind the line of scrimmage. If he threw an incomplete pass, his team was penalized five yards! If he threw an incomplete pass into the end zone, it was called a "touchback," and the ball went to the other team!

Downs. Early on in pro ball, a team had three "downs" to advance the ball—but they only had to go five yards (4.6 m) to get a first down. This rule was changed in 1912. Teams were allowed four downs instead of three, but the ball had to be advanced ten yards (9.1 m) to get a first down.

Kickoff. In the first years of the game, the ball was kicked off from the middle of the field, the 50-yard line. In 1912, this was changed to the 40-yard line. But in 1924, the placement was again put in the middle of the field. Later, this was changed to the 35-yard line, then to the 30, as today. Whew!

From "Iron Man" to "Platoon" Football

For the first 30 years of pro football, players on a team played both offense and defense. This was called "Iron Man" football. One of the greatest "Iron Men" was Sammy Baugh of the Washington Redskins. For much of his career, Baugh was the best defensive back, quarterback, and punter in pro football.

"Iron Man" football began to wane in the 1940s, when the "free substitution" rule was adopted. Fresh players constantly came in and out of the game. In the 1950s, pro teams quit playing two-way "Iron Man" football.

Sammy Baugh, "Iron Man" of the Washington Redskins

Instead, entire platoons of players were sent in, depending on the team's needs and circumstances. Each player (and his platoon) specialized in offense, defense, or special teams (punts, kickoffs, and extra points).

The Stadiums

Often, football games were played in all sorts of crazy places. For example, an important playoff game in 1928 was played at the Providence, Rhode Island Cycledrome. The arena had originally been built for bicycle races. In 1932, the championship game was between the Chicago Bears and Portsmouth Spartans. Chicago was snowbound and the temperature was 30 degrees below zero Fahrenheit. Due to the bad weather, the game was moved indoors to Chicago Stadium and played on a layer of dirt spread on concrete. The field was 20 yards (18.3 m) too short and 10 yards (9.1 m) too narrow.

In the early stadiums, the stands were just a few feet from the sidelines. Hard to believe, but there were often no benches for the players. The players sat right alongside the fans in the front row!

Pro Ball—On the Air

In the 1920s, before the days of electronic media coverage of sports, the fans of most teams did not learn whether their team had won or lost until the next day's newspaper came out.

Green Bay Packer fans were not about to wait. Instead, when the Packers went on the road, as many as 500 fans would go to a park in the middle of town to follow the game. Fans who went on the road with the team would phone in whenever there was a score, and at the end of a quarter. An "announcer" at the park would then relay the information to the fans gathered there.

During the 1930s, local radio stations started covering games. Whether

Radio announcers of the 1930s covering a game

the team was at home or away, fans could listen to the play-by-play
broadcasts in their hometowns.

A Thanksgiving Day showdown between Chicago and Detroit in
November of 1934 was a turning point in NFL history. The game, which was
won by the Bears in the final minutes, was the first NFL game to be aired on
radio for a national audience. People all over the country were able to tune
into the action, which was carried live on the NBC radio network.

The 1940s—Pro Ball in the World War II Era

The war had a great impact on pro football. Many players joined the
military and the rosters of teams were depleted. During the 1943 season,
the Pittsburgh Steelers and Philadelphia Eagles merged into one team, the
Phil-Pit Steagles, because neither team had enough players to exist on its
own. The following year, in 1944, in the Chicago Cardinals and the Steelers
joined for one season and formed the pro team of Card-Pitt.

During the war years, all players were required to work at least 40 hours a week in defense plants. Then, they would train for three hours each night, from 6 P.M. to 9 P.M. Said one player of the time, Jack Hinkle: "You worked all day, and you practiced football all night. By the end of the day, you were [so tired] you could hardly move."

Did You Know?

More than 600 players and coaches fought in the war. Twenty-one of them died on the battlefield.

Shattering the Race Barrier

Fritz Pollard was the first African American to play pro football. This was back in 1916. Still, in those early years of the game there were almost no black players.

In 1947, Jackie Robinson was signed by baseball's Brooklyn Dodgers. A year earlier, in 1946, four African Americans had been drafted into the NFL. Two were from UCLA, and both played for the L.A. Rams. In addition to so much else, the 1940s was a decade in which racial barriers in sports began to fall.

A New League

In 1944, the All-America Football Conference (AAFC) was formed. Though the NFL would have nothing to do with the teams in this conference at first, the AAFC, nevertheless, fielded teams. The original AAFC teams were the Buffalo Bisons, the Brooklyn Dodgers, the New York Yankees, the

Cleveland Browns, the Los Angeles Dons, the Miami Seahawks, the Chicago Rockets, and the San Francisco 49ers. Eventually, three AAFC teams would join the NFL: the 49ers, Browns, and a new team, the Baltimore Colts.

The 1950s—the Golden Age of the NFL

The 1950s were the turning point for the NFL. The game had been getting better and more exciting each year. Just as important was TV. It was only in black-and-white back then, but the games were broadcast on coast-to-coast television. Suddenly, all of America was watching pro football. This included the West Coast. The Rams had moved from Cleveland to Los Angeles in 1946, and the San Francisco 49ers had been absorbed from the old AAFC.

A November 1950 football game between the L.A. Rams and the N.Y. Yankees

Early on, teams traveled by bus or train to games away from home. Travel by airplane began in the late 1940s; by the 1950s, flying became the standard way for squads to get quickly and easily to away-game sites.

In 1950, the L.A. Rams became the first team to televise both its home and away games. This was a mistake. With home games on TV, fans stayed away from the Coliseum.

In 1951, the Rams switched to televising only away games. Soon, this became the standard for the NFL. Attendance at home games rose tremendously.

In 1952, the Dallas Texans entered the NFL. They did poorly at first; in 1963, they moved and became the Kansas City Chiefs.

The 1960s—The Great Merger

This decade marked the addition of four new football teams: Dallas, Minnesota, Atlanta, and New Orleans joined the NFL.

Since the late 1940s, all teams played a 12-game schedule. In 1961, this was changed to 14 games.

The idea for another football league began with a 1959 meeting of prospective team owners. By the 1960s, this new league, the American Football League (AFL), became a reality. In 1966, the teams from the AFL joined the NFL. After the merger, the NFL owners divided the league into two conferences, The NFC (National Football Conference) and the AFC (American Football Conference). The winners of the two conferences met for the World Championship Game at the end of each season. In 1968, the Championship Game became the Super Bowl.

Did You Know?

The Cleveland Browns named themselves after their coach, Paul Brown, the only team to do so.

The 1970s—Let 'Em Fly!

The 1970s began as an era of awesome defenses facing offenses geared to a grinding running game. Fans preferred the excitement of the pass—and lots of scoring. But scoring was the lowest it had been since 1942. As a result, attendance began falling. However, by the end of the decade, the passes were flying—and the fans were flocking back to see quarterbacks like Ken Stabler (Raiders) and Terry Bradshaw (Steelers) light up the scoreboard.

This was an era of great teams. The Pittsburgh Steelers won four Super Bowls. The Dallas Cowboys won 105 games and lost only 39. Miami won five of ten division titles, and had a perfect 17—0 season in 1972. The Minnesota Vikings took eight of ten games.

These outstanding offensive performances were partly the result of changes in the rules. Before this time, defenders had used a head slap to knock players out of the way in order to get to the quarterback. In 1977, the "head slap" was outlawed. In 1978, offensive linemen were given the freedom to use open hands and extended arms on pass blocks. The penalty for holding (illegal use of the hands to hold an opponent in place) was reduced from 15 yards to 10 (13.7 m to 9.1).

There were other changes that made the game more exciting, too. To avoid ties as much as possible, a 15-minute "sudden death" overtime period was added to regular games. Only if a game was still tied after this one 15-minute period would it be recorded as a tie. In championship games, however, there couldn't be any ties. As many extra periods as needed were played until one team scored the winning points.

"Monday Night Football" was another addition to the sport that made it more thrilling and popular during the 1970s. The first game shown took place on September 21, 1970, with the Cleveland Browns beating the New York Jets

31—21. Eighty-five thousand fans were in the stadium, and millions more watched on TV.

The 1980s—On the Move!

By the 1980s, pro football had become the most popular spectator sport in the United States. Still, trouble loomed ahead. Twice during the 1980s, regular season games were canceled because of players' strikes. Players wanted higher salaries, improved benefits, and "free agency," the right to go

Pro players on strike

to another team if they were dissatisfied with their contracts.

During this decade, many teams moved to new cities. The L.A. Rams moved to Anaheim, California. The Oakland Raiders filled the vacancy and moved to L.A. The St. Louis Cardinals became the Phoenix Cardinals. The Colts galloped from Baltimore to Indianapolis.

Meanwhile, the 49ers stayed put in San Francisco. Behind the passing combination of Joe Montana and Jerry Rice, the 49ers were the team of the decade, winning four Super Bowls.

The 1983 football draft (when teams chose new players) is unequaled in NFL history. Among other greats, this draft yielded John Elway (Denver Broncos), Jim Kelly (Buffalo Bills), and Dan Marino (Miami Dolphins). The same year, NFL running backs slashed through defenses. Sixteen rushers gained a thousand or more yards. Included in this Who's Who of NFL runners are Eric Dickerson, Walter Payton, John Riggins, Earl Campbell, Marcus Allen, and Franco Harris. The 1980s also saw the birth of another phenomenon—the 300-pound lineman.

Instant Replay. In 1986, the NFL began experimenting with "instant replay." An official sat in a booth in front of two TV monitors. He could play back the game's action in slow-motion, and reverse a call made by a field umpire if film footage showed an error had been made. Because instant replay slowed down the action, it was abandoned in 1992. It was brought back in 1998, but each team was limited to a maximum of only six "challenges" per game.

The USFL. The United States Football League entered the picture in 1983 with teams such as the Houston Gamblers, Chicago Blitz, and Memphis Showboats. The games were played from March through July, during the off-season for the NFL (which plays from September through January). The idea was to offer fans year-round football. It flopped, and the USFL folded in 1986.

The 1990s—Into the Space Age

The 1990s was an era of new teams. Among these were the Carolina Panthers, the Jacksonville Jaguars, and the Baltimore Ravens.

It was also a time when many teams moved to new cities, often with strange results. The Rams, after having just run off from L.A. to nearby Anaheim a few years before, headed for St. Louis, Missouri. The Browns went from Cleveland to Baltimore, but had to leave their name behind, so that a new Cleveland "Browns" could be formed. The team in Baltimore adopted the name "Ravens." The Houston Oilers slipped off to Tennessee. But instead of being called the Oilers, the Tennessee team wanted to be the Titans.

There were "Space Age" additions to uniforms. One of these was the plastic face shield, the first of which was made for a linebacker with an injured eye. Then came tinted shields, which also served as huge, weird sunglasses. Mouthpieces caught on during this time, too.

In the 1990s, receivers started wearing golf gloves to give them a better grip on the ball. Soon, there were custom-made "football gloves"—with different designs for different positions.

Air-cushioned shoulder pads and helmets were hits of this decade. One experimental helmet had a pump inside, and a player could fix the fit right on the field.

The "TV helmet" was a more exotic experiment. A small camera placed in the quarterback's headgear gave TV viewers an insanely up-close view of the action.

Even more bizarre was a microphone installed in the quarterback's helmet. Barking out signals. Yelling. Heaving breathing. Cursing. Fans heard it all, as everything coming from the quarterback's mouth was broadcast over loudspeakers in the stands.

Other '90s stuff:

◆ In 1994, the NFL adopted the two-point conversion after a touchdown. This gave teams the choice between kicking for one point or trying to get into the end zone to score two points.

◆ In 1933, the average salary for a pro player was $8,000. By the 1950s it was only up to $10,000; and most players had off-season jobs to make ends meet. But by the end of the millennium, the average salary of a football player was over half a million dollars a year.

◆ TV and "free agency" are the two reasons pro athletes—in basketball and baseball, as well as football—make so much money. TV stations pay the

NFL owners billions of dollars for the rights to show the games. Because of the "free-agency" rule, players can sell their talent to the highest bidder (i.e., the owner willing to pay the most money). As a result, team rosters change constantly. In 1993, a fourth of all pro players put on the uniform of an "enemy" team.

1992: World League football coach and players for Spain's Barcelona Dragons

The Future

Pro football has gone through endless changes. More will surely come in the future.

One idea is the elimination of the huddle. Instead, players would communicate with each other through radio receivers (an idea that had first been tried by Paul Brown in the 1950s).

Another idea is global football. On August 3, 1984, the Bears and Cowboys met in London, England, for the first NFL game in a foreign city. The Bears beat the Cowboys 17—6 in front of more than 82,000 spectators in London's Wembley Stadium. Since then, there have been preseason games played in Berlin, Tokyo, and Montreal.

The World Football League was formed in 1991. Of the ten teams, three were from European cities—the Barcelona Dragons, the London Monarchs, and the Frankfurt Galaxy. From Canada came the Montreal Machine. Rounding out the list were six teams from U.S. cities. The WFL went out of business in 1993. Still, it was a taste of things to come. It is probably only a matter of time before pro football is played worldwide.

CONCLUSION

During the last century, three uniquely American sports evolved. The history of these sports—baseball, basketball, and football—is fascinating. Undoubtedly, it will be equally intriguing to see how the games change in this next century.

In basketball, for example, will it be commonplace to see players that are eight feet (2.4 m) tall? And as a result, will the baskets be raised from ten feet to twelve feet (3.1 m to 3.7 m), or perhaps even higher, as some people have suggested?

In baseball, will the outfield fences be moved closer to home plate so that more home runs can be hit? And, to speed up the action and make the game higher scoring, will players get a "walk" on only three bad pitches (instead of four)?

And what about football? Will the players wear uniforms that look like space suits? Will there be football teams all over the world—in Europe, Asia, and Africa?

What the future holds for football, basketball, and baseball is going to be interesting to see. At present, it's anybody's guess—including yours—what will happen. In your opinion, how could these sports be made even more fun, exciting, and enjoyable—to both play and watch? What changes do you envision for these sports in the years ahead?